Scrum Insights
for Practitioners

Scrum Insights for Practitioners

THE SCRUM GUIDE COMPANION

• • •

Hiren Doshi

ISBN: 0692807179
ISBN 13: 9780692807170

Contents

To my
wonderful parents;
beautiful wife, Swati; and
loving daughters, Aditi and Ashwini.

Foreword by Gunther Verheyen

• • •

SCRUM GREW LESS AND LESS complete and "perfect" over time. Practices and techniques were gradually removed from the official definition of Scrum in *The Scrum Guide*. As the global Scrum adoption grew and Scrum became the most adopted method for Agile software development, more and more space was created for variation in techniques and practices by eliminating specific instructions from the official body of knowledge of Scrum. Scrum turned into the framework that it was always designed to be, a framework that enables practitioners to devise their own solutions.

In his book *Scrum Insights for Practitioners*, Hiren has extended the core rules of *The Scrum Guide* with practices he has found useful. Hiren answers questions regarding Scrum that potentially remain unanswered even after one reads *The Scrum Guide*. Hiren dismantles common misconceptions about Scrum, regardless of the source of such misconceptions. Hiren elaborates on basic information provided in *The Scrum Guide*, as well as on the principles underlying Scrum.

Hiren shows that experts understand that there are still many people new to Scrum looking for help and guidance, people who might not have the possibility to learn through extensive experience. Hiren respects people looking for information additional to *The Scrum Guide*, without ever turning any of his advice, practices, or insights into "must" prescriptions.

Reading *The Scrum Guide* and additionally reading *Scrum Insights for Practitioners* provides any aspiring Scrum practitioner with valuable base insights, without leaving the impression it can replace actual experience.

Enjoy reading. Keep Scrumming.

Gunther Verheyen
Independent Scrum Caretaker
Antwerp
September 22, 2016

Recommendations

• • •

"One of the best things about Scrum is its simplicity. It's very easy to get started using Scrum, but if you're not careful, you can make a lot of mistakes. Take advantage of Hiren's vast experience and avoid making the common errors people make as they begin their journey. This book contains a wealth of practical information that will be useful to readers as they work to implement the basic theory found in *The Scrum Guide*." —Steve Porter, team member, Scrum.org

"Hiren Doshi has written a fine companion to *The Scrum Guide*, filling in some of the intentional gaps left in the Scrum framework. Using this companion along with *The Scrum Guide* will undoubtedly improve the outlook for those teams that internalize its teachings." —Charles Bradley, ScrumCrazy.com

"This book will help you understand the nuances of Scrum. It takes a very practical approach toward implementing Scrum without compromising on its values and principles. Perhaps the first book on Scrum that newbies should read after going through *The Scrum Guide*. A useful and handy reference for Scrum practitioners!"—Gopinath R., Agile coach and practitioner

Acknowledgments

• • •

I'M INCREDIBLY HONORED AND PRIVILEGED to have the best Scrum experts in the industry as the official reviewers of my first book. I owe a tremendous debt to Steve Porter, Gunther Verheyen, and Charles Bradley for reading and providing their expert comments on the manuscript. Each of them has provided valuable insights to make my writing more complete. Thank you.

Very special thanks to Gopinath Ramakrishnan, a good friend and a Scrum expert himself, for reviewing and editing the manuscript during my early days of writing and providing me with valuable insights. Thank you for being patient with me and helping me improve the manuscript.

Thank you, Gunther Verheyen, for writing such a fantastic foreword. I am honored.

Thank you, Ken Schwaber and Jeff Sutherland, for teaching me Scrum.

Finally, a thank-you to my wife, Swati, for reviewing the book and giving her valuable insights. I also thank her for always being there for me throughout the journey. Thank you!

Preface

• • •

SCRUM IS A FRAMEWORK TO manage complex product development. The framework consists of three roles, five formal events, three artifacts, and the rules that bind these elements together. *The Scrum Guide* is the one and only official description of Scrum and is freely available at ScrumGuides.org. *The Scrum Guide* is written and maintained by the cocreators of Scrum, Ken Schwaber and Jeff Sutherland.

The Scrum Guide holds the bare and essential rules of Scrum. It provides sufficient information to understand Scrum but leaves much open for interpretation by readers and practitioners. When individuals and organizations follow *The Scrum Guide* blindly, without understanding the real, deep essence of Scrum—the principles and values underpinning the framework—they likely will fail to reap all the benefits Scrum has to offer.

As noted in *The Scrum Guide*, Scrum can be compared to the game of chess: easy to understand but difficult to master. Why? As in the game of chess, the rules of the game are very simple, but the game has millions of strategies by which it can be played. How many grand masters do we know who have mastered chess?

Most likely we will be able to count the names on the fingers of our hands.

Ten years back, I started my Agile software development journey via Scrum. I began my practice for a large organization in the United States by just reading *The Scrum Guide*. I enjoyed every moment of the journey, and I was under the impression that I was doing a fabulous job with the Scrum adoption in the organization. Luckily, six months into the adoption, I started attending Ken Schwaber's Scrum-But sessions, held in his Burlington, Massachusetts, office. These sessions were eye-openers for me as I realized that I did not really have a deep understanding of what Scrum is and the way it is supposed to be practiced. In fact, it was much worse than that: I had not just limited my muddied understanding of Scrum to myself, but I had distributed this knowledge to many others who collaborated with me on product development.

Scrum Insights for Practitioners fills in some gaps in the understanding of Scrum for individuals or organizations practicing Scrum. This book can be thought of as a companion to *The Scrum Guide*. I encourage readers to first read *The Scrum Guide* if you are new to Scrum before reading this book, as this will help you reap the maximum benefits.

Scrum Insights for Practitioners is a perfect companion to *The Scrum Guide* that helps the practitioners master the Scrum framework by gaining in-depth practical insights and helps answer questions such as these:

- What are some common myths, mysteries, and misconceptions of Scrum?
- *The Scrum Guide* recommends three to nine members in a Development Team, but we have fifteen members. Is this Scrum?
- Can you share some tactics to do effective Sprint Planning, Daily Scrum, Sprint Review, Sprint Retrospective, and Product Backlog Refinement?
- My designation is development manager. Does this mean I have no role in Scrum?
- How is Scrum Empirical?
- Can Scrum Master and Product Owner be the same person?
- We don't have a Scrum Master. Are we still practicing Scrum?
- What does self-organization really mean?
- How does Scrum embrace the four values and twelve principles of the Agile Manifesto?
- Please share a case study on Scrum-based product development?

This book is a collection of my experiences and learning and will provide you guidance and suggestions about adopting Scrum. It will also help clear up the myths and misconceptions of Scrum. Each organization's business context varies, and it is very difficult to prescribe a best practice that will work for everyone. You are in a better position to understand the exact circumstances of your business needs and adapt accordingly.

Scrum Theory and Definition of Scrum

• • •

WHAT IS SCRUM?

AS DEFINED IN *THE SCRUM Guide,* Scrum is a lightweight framework founded on empirical process control theory that supports small teams in addressing complex adaptive problems while productively and creatively delivering products of the highest possible value.

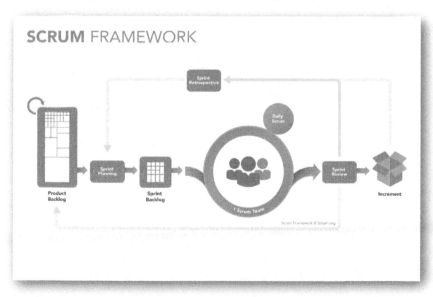

An alternative definition of Scrum

Scrum is an **iterative** way of developing software in a Sprint (a time-box of one month or less), **incrementally delivering** working software every Sprint, incorporating customer **feedback** on the working software, and ensuring that the right **business value** is delivered in each Sprint.

What Is a Complex Adaptive Problem?

According to the Cynefin framework, by David Snowden, any software project that you pick up can be bucketed in one of four categories:

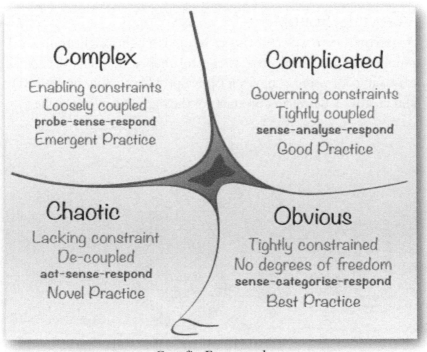

Cynefin Framework
By Snowded, 2014, Last modified July 6 2014. https://commons.wikimedia.org/w/index.php?curid=33783436.

* Obvious: Everything about the project is known.
* Complicated: More about the project is known than is unknown.
* Complex: More about the project is unknown than is known.
* Chaotic: Everything is unknown. There is no proven approach.

Each category requires a different approach:

Projects in the Obvious and Complicated domains can follow a predictive model—plan driven or waterfall—and a project plan can be put in place as most of the requirements, the technology, and people aspects of the projects are well known in advance and hold few uncertainties.

Example 1: Rewriting an existing payroll application.

Example 2: Building a sea link using a suspended bridge to connect two cities. Although this might not sound like a simple, uncomplicated project, it actually is. Humans have been building bridges for centuries, and we have accumulated plenty of data on the same. The data can be analyzed to put a solid plan together, and most likely one can comfortably predict the time and cost needed to build a bridge with no more than 5 to 10 percent variance on the planned work.

If we are very certain about the project requirements and the technology we plan to use, it is well proven that a predictive model is a better choice.

For Chaotic projects no defined process works, as almost everything about the project is unknown and is subject to extensive changes. The best model for such projects is to act in order to establish some type of direction and then decide on the next move.

Software projects reside in the Complex domain, as it is extremely difficult to envision the exact final outcome of the product and how the market will embrace it when it is released. Products and services like Uber, Apple, Google, Amazon, and Facebook have evolved over time. The founders of these companies most likely did not envision the exact products that we use today when they conceived the first ideas. The complexity in software arises from these facts: there are many unknown variables, and for known variables the variance is too much.

These are some of the variables that make software development complex:

1. Requirements: Software requirements never stop changing. The customer often will not know what he or she wants until the customer can actually use the product.
2. Technology: This is an ever-changing variable.
3. People: The people aspect is very unpredictable (e.g., attrition, leaves of absence, skill gaps).

For complex projects, empirical process control, or empiricism, is the best-suited approach.

What Is Empirical Process Control, or Empiricism?

Empiricism means working in a fact-based, experience-based, and evidence-based manner. Scrum implements an empirical process where progress is based on observations of reality, not fictitious plans.

Here is an analogy to explain empiricism:

Assume you need to develop twenty-five equally sized features for a product before it can be released to the market. You agree to develop five features in each one-month Sprint. This means you will complete twenty-five features in five Sprints—that is, five features delivered by the end of each one-month Sprint.

Suppose you complete seven features in the first Sprint instead of the planned five. This evidence of your real progress gives you the insight that you can take on more features in the next Sprint— that is, seven features instead of the planned five. This also means that the project might turn out to be much simpler than you anticipated, and instead of five Sprints to complete all twenty-five features, you might end up needing only four Sprints.

Suppose, however, that you complete only two features instead of the planned five in the first Sprint. This evidence of actual progress gives you the insight that you had better take on fewer features in the next Sprint—that is, two features instead of the planned five. This also means that the project might turn out to be more difficult than you anticipated. Instead of five Sprints to complete all twenty-five features, you might need over twelve Sprints.

If you are not able to complete any features in a Sprint, then you still come away with the insight that you might need to slice and plan your work in a very different way.

Thus, real data enable good decision making in a timely manner. Contrast this with a traditional predictive model—like waterfall—where sponsors spend huge amounts of money without knowing the outcome for a very long period, often years. Scrum, due to its empirical nature, is very appealing to sponsors as at the end of each Sprint, a potentially releasable "Done" Product Increment is available. The increment can be inspected and potentially released if deemed sufficiently valuable every one month or less.

The Three Pillars of Empiricism (Scrum)

Scrum is empirical and places great emphasis on mind-set and cultural shift to achieve business and organizational Agility. The three pillars of empirical process control are as follows:

* **Transparency**: This means presenting the facts as is. All people involved—the customer, the CEO, individual contributors—are transparent in their day-to-day dealings with others. They all trust each other, and they have the courage to keep each other abreast of good news as well as bad news. Everyone strives and collectively collaborates for the common organizational objective, and no one has any hidden agenda.
* **Inspection**: Inspection in this context is not an inspection by an inspector or an auditor but an inspection by everyone on the Scrum Team. The inspection can be done for

the product, processes, people aspects, practices, and continuous improvements. For example, the team openly and transparently shows the product at the end of each Sprint to the customer in order to gather valuable feedback. If the customer changes the requirements during inspection, the team does not complain but rather adapts by using this as an opportunity to collaborate with the customer to clarify the requirements and test out the new hypothesis.

* **Adaptation**: Adaptation in this context is about continuous improvement, the ability to adapt based on the results of the inspection. Everyone in the organization must ask this question regularly: Are we better off than yesterday? For profit-based organizations, the value is represented in terms of profit. The adaptation should eventually relay back to one of the reasons for adapting Agile—for example, faster time to market, increased return on investment through value-based delivery, reduced total cost of ownership through enhanced software quality, and improved customer and employee satisfaction.

Scrum works not because it has three roles, five events, and three artifacts but because it adheres to the underlying Agile principles of iterative, value-based incremental delivery by frequently gathering customer feedback and embracing change. This results in faster time to market, better delivery predictability, increased customer responsiveness, ability to change direction by managing changing priorities, enhanced software quality, and improved risk management.

The Scrum Values

• • •

THE SCRUM PILLARS OF TRANSPARENCY, inspection, and adaptation come to life and build trust for everyone when the Scrum values are embodied and lived by everyone. The Scrum values are courage, focus, commitment, respect, and openness.

Successful use of Scrum depends on people becoming more proficient in adapting their behavior to these five Scrum values. Gunther Verheyen has captured the values very well on his blog:

Gunther, V. (May 2015). https://guntherverheyen.com/2013/05/03/theres-value-in-the-scrum-values/

Scrum Values

This is my interpretation and adaptation of his text:

COURAGE

The Scrum Team members have the courage to do the right thing and collaborate on difficult problems. They show courage in being transparent and sharing risks and benefits as they are. They admit that requirements will never be close to perfect and show courage not only by acknowledging that but also by adapting to changing requirements and direction. They show courage in admitting that nobody is perfect and accepting people for who they are. The Scrum Team shows the courage to promote Scrum and empiricism to deal with complexity.

FOCUS

Everyone focuses on the work of the Sprint and the goals of the Scrum Team. The time-boxes of Scrum allow a Scrum Team to focus on delivering valuable working software at a sustainable pace. The team focuses on simplicity (e.g., no gold plating) and delivering to the needs of the customer. The team focuses on embedding good engineering practices for Lean software development and increased value and quality delivery.

COMMITMENT

People personally commit to achieving the goals of the Scrum Team. They commit to the Agile values and principles as documented in the Agile Manifesto. The Scrum Team commits to building working software, to quality, to collaborating, to learning, to self-organizing, to building the right thing for its customers, to excelling, to being creative and innovating, to continuously improving upon regular inspections and adaptations, to the Scrum framework, to transparency, and to challenging the status quo.

RESPECT

Scrum Team members respect each other to be capable and independent people. They show respect for people. They respect diversity. They respect the Scrum roles, rules, and principles. They show respect by building valuable, releasable-quality working software with every Sprint.

OPENNESS

The Scrum Team and its stakeholders agree to be open about all the work and the challenges with performing the work. They are open to collaborating within the team and with the organization. They are open to being transparent.

The Scrum Team

. . .

A Scrum Team has three roles:

* The Product Owner
* The Scrum Master
* The Development Team

The various levels of service and their responsibilities in the Scrum Team are as follows:

* The Scrum Master serves the Development Team and the Product Owner.
* The Development Team serves the Product Owner.
* The Product Owner serves the stakeholders.

The Product Owner

* The Product Owner in Scrum is an entrepreneur—a value maximizer and optimizer. The Product Owner ensures that the Development Team works on the most valuable

functionality first. The primary tool for a Product Owner to do so is the ordered Product Backlog.

* The Product Owner is a product manager. To maximize the value of the product, the Product Owner needs awareness of competitive research, product vision, forecasting and feasibility, road mapping, return on investment, total cost of ownership, and so forth.

* The Product Owner sets a solid vision to help the Scrum Team keep a laser-sharp focus and direction that helps with incremental progress.

* One product has only one Product Backlog and only one Product Owner. Having one Product Owner for the product maximizes clarity and focus, ensures quick decision making, and eliminates wasteful delays by making a single person accountable for the success of the product.

* To validate the idea, the Product Owner frequently releases the software increment to market to gain real customer insights.

* The Product Owner is accountable for and has the final say on the ordering of the Product Backlog. The Product Owner orders the Product Backlog items (PBI) in the Product Backlog by balancing many parameters, such as the value of a PBI, the dependencies between PBIs, and dependencies on other products.
    * Value realized can be determined by the following:
        * Revenue for profit-based organizations (e.g., Amazon, Apple, Google)
        * Benefits to society by not-for-profit organizations (e.g., American Red Cross, UNICEF, BRAC, CARE)

* Value in itself is hard to quantify, but KPIs can be used to measure how effective we are in delivering value. Some metrics to measure value are defined in the framework of evidence-based management for software organizations available through http://www.ebmgt.org:
    * Feature Usage Index: How much functionality of the product is being utilized?
    * Installed Version Index: What percentage of your customers is on your latest release?
    * Innovation Rate: What percentage of your product budget is spent on building new functionality versus maintaining existing functionality versus expanding capabilities?
    * On-Product Index: What percentage of team time is spent working on product and value?
    * Time to market, customer satisfaction, impact on revenue, and impact on cost are some other metrics that the Product Owner might use frequently to determine a product's success.
* The Product Owner, as the owner of a product, is accountable not only for development and release of the product but also for the cost of maintaining and operating the product: the total cost of ownership (TCO).
* For the Product Owner to succeed, the entire organization must respect his or her decisions. No one is allowed to tell the Development Team to work from a different set of requirements, and the Development Team is not allowed to act on what anyone else says.
* The Product Owner will help adjust the Sprint scope in case the Development Team has overcommitted itself for the Sprint.

* The writing of acceptance criteria for the Product Backlog item is a collaborative exercise between the Product Owner and the Development Team.
    * The Product Owner builds trust by closely working with the Development Team. He or she is not hesitant to delegate the work of writing the PBI to the Development Team.
* It is important to understand that the Development Team can pick up a PBI even if complete acceptance criteria are not specified. This happens as long as enough understanding exists between the Development Team and the Product Owner.
* The Product Owner ensures that all work done by the Development Team originates from the single Product Backlog, the single source of truth.
* During the actual Sprint, the Product Owner is accountable for the following:
    * Product Backlog refinement, but he or she may delegate the work to the Development Team
    * Interacting and engaging with the stakeholders
* The Product Owner focuses more on desired outcomes and not features or implementation and encourages the Development Team to work directly with the stakeholders and users for clarifications on a PBI so he or she does not become a bottleneck.
* Only the Product Owner has the authority to cancel a Sprint, although he or she may do so under influence from the stakeholders, the Development Team, or the Scrum Master. This generally happens when the Sprint goal becomes obsolete or no longer makes sense.
    * When a Sprint is canceled, any completed and "Done" PBIs are reviewed. If part of the work is potentially

releasable, the Product Owner typically accepts it. All incomplete PBIs are reestimated and put back on the Product Backlog.
* The Product Owner is just one person and not a committee.
* A "cone of uncertainty" (i.e., best, worst, average estimates based on past progress on the Product Backlog) helps the Product Owner forecast how much work is likely to be done during a certain number of Sprints based on the empirical evidence from previous Sprints.
* To minimize waste in developing and sustaining the Product Backlog, the Product Owner ensures the following:
  * A PBI is detailed only when it seems sure it is likely to be implemented.
  * A PBI is written clearly and with as little ambiguity as possible.

The Scrum Master

* The Scrum Master is accountable for building high-performing Scrum Teams.
* The primary responsibility of the Scrum Master is to educate teams and the organization on Scrum values, theory, practices, and rules. The Scrum Master is accountable for the way Scrum is understood and enacted.
* A Scrum Master's role is that of coach, teacher, mentor, and facilitator. The Scrum Master as a servant-leader does these roles by being invisibly present.

* The Scrum Master is responsible for removing impediments. And the best way a Scrum Master can remove impediments is to empower, teach, and coach the Development Team to remove impediments themselves. Only if the team is stuck should the Scrum Master remove the impediments himself or herself.
* To encourage self-organization, the Scrum Master guides the team to solve its own problems by using the three pillars of empiricism and facilitating Development Team decisions.
* The Scrum Master uses facilitation as a management tool, including techniques like open questions and active listening.
* The Scrum Master engages the Scrum Team by reminding them of the organization's purpose and vision.
* The Scrum Master is always on a lookout for opportunities to educate the Development Team in identifying and eliminating waste to make the process Lean, thereby imbibing a culture of Agility within the organization.
* The Scrum Master mentors the team to focus on value, flow, and quality.
* To foster better communication between the Development Team and Product Owner, the Scrum Master teaches the Development Team to talk to the Product Owner in terms of business needs and objectives.
* The Scrum Master is responsible for ensuring an effective Daily Scrum happens every day and is time-boxed to fifteen minutes even though he or she is an optional attendee in the Daily Scrum.

The Development Team

* The Development Team self-organizes and self-manages its work for the Sprint.
* The Development Team alone is responsible for delivering a Product Increment at the end of every Sprint. The Product Owner helps ensure the value of the increment by ordering the Product Backlog. The Scrum Master helps create value by ensuring that the Scrum process is enacted.
* The Development Team is accountable for the quality of the deliverable by building a releasable software increment that adheres to its agreed definition of "Done" at the end of every Sprint.
* The Development Team is responsible for resolving any internal conflicts on its own. If needed, it may accept help from the Scrum Master.
* The Development Team determines how the work must be performed throughout every Sprint.
* The Development Team pulls the work from the Product Backlog. Nobody can push work to the Development Team. Only the Development Team can determine how many PBIs must be pulled from the Product Backlog.
* The Development Team must have the knowledge and skill set needed to deliver an increment that meets the definition of "Done" at the end of the Sprint.
* The ownership of the Sprint Backlog item lies with the entire Development Team and not a particular individual.
* The Development Team is responsible for estimating the PBIs. The Product Owner may influence the Development

Team by helping its members understand and select trade-offs, but the Development Team, who will perform the work, must make the final estimate.

* The Development Team alone is responsible for tracking the progress of the work remaining in the Sprint to achieve the forecasted Sprint goal.

* The Development Team is responsible for the definition of "Done," including incorporating quality expectations provided by the organization. The Product Owner may be consulted and might influence the definition of "Done," but the Development Team is responsible.

* Everyone in the Development Team is responsible for the quality, and there is no "tester" role in a Development Team.

* If an additional Scrum Team is added to the product being developed, the productivity of the original Scrum Team normally decreases owing to the effort spent on resolving dependencies and integration issues.

* The Development Team membership can change as needed, taking into account a short-term reduction in productivity. Ideally, team members are added or removed only between Sprints and not while a Sprint is in progress.

* The Development Team informs the Product Owner to work with anyone that requests to add new PBI to a Sprint that is currently ongoing.

* The Product Owner and the Scrum Master can be part of the Development Team, if they are also executing the work of the Sprint Backlog.

* The Development Team can be constructed in many ways. Nevertheless, all teams have to prepare and present one

integrated increment that adheres to the agreed common definition of "Done" at the end of the Sprint. The teams can be formed as follows:

* Cross-functional or feature teams: Each team must be able to deliver complete functionality across all layers (e.g., data, logic, presentation) of the product and the shared architecture in each Sprint. *The Scrum Guide* recommends that Development Teams be cross-functional by having cross-skilled individuals who are able to contribute according to their skills and competencies to produce a working "Done" software increment.

* Component teams: There is a layer-wise distribution of architectural work among the teams, and some processes are defined for maintaining the shared system. For example, teams of UI expertise or database expertise can be formed. But teams must understand the overhead in terms of dependencies and integration challenges to build a potentially releasable "Done" increment at the end of each Sprint.

DEVELOPMENT TEAM SIZE

The recommended size of the Development Team—excluding the Product Owner and Scrum Master unless they are working off the Sprint Backlog, as suggested by *The Scrum Guide*—is three to nine members. You are still doing Scrum if you form a Development Team with two members or less, or nine members or more, as long as you understand the results will be suboptimal.

THE AVAILABILITY OF THE THREE ROLES

As *The Scrum Guide* advises, the Scrum Team *must* have three roles: the Scrum Master, the Product Owner, and the Development Team.

SHOULD THE SCRUM MASTER BE ON THE SCRUM TEAM FULL TIME?

* Scrum prescribes a role called Scrum Master. In the absence of a Scrum Master, you are not doing Scrum.
* The Scrum Master must be 100 percent committed to the Scrum Team but does not have to be full time on the Scrum Team. As long as the Scrum Master can do justice to his or her role, he or she can serve multiple Scrum Teams or get operationally engaged by working part time as a Development Team member.

SHOULD THE PRODUCT OWNER BE ON THE SCRUM TEAM FULL TIME?

* Scrum prescribes a role called Product Owner. The Product Owner is responsible for maximizing the value of the product and the work of the Development Team. In the absence of a Product Owner, there is no accountability for the latter, and you are not doing Scrum.
* The Product Owner must be 100 percent committed to the Scrum Team but does not have to be full time on the Scrum Team. As long as the Product Owner can do justice to his or her role, serve the team, and interact with the stakeholders, he or she can serve multiple Scrum Teams

or get operationally engaged by working part time as a Development Team member. Remember, one product has only one Product Backlog and only one Product Owner.

SHOULD THE DEVELOPMENT TEAM MEMBERS ON THE SCRUM TEAM BE FULL TIME?

* The Development Team members must be 100 percent committed to the Scrum Team but do not have to be on the Development Team full time. For example, data-tuning expertise might be scarce in the organization. In a particular Sprint, five Scrum Teams might be looking for a data-tuning expert, but the organization has only one person with this skill. If the data-tuning expert works as a full-time Development Team member for a particular Scrum Team, the other teams will be starved and most likely will not be able to accomplish their goals for the Sprint. In such situations there are multiple options that can be tried. I am listing a few:
    * The data-tuning expert may become a consultant to the Scrum Teams, and the Development Team might schedule time to work with the expert.
    * The Scrum Team might decide to carve out a new Scrum Team with select members from all Scrum Teams and pair up with the data-tuning expert. This allows cross skill training, and the members can bring the new learnings back to their respective Scrum Teams.

CAN THE SAME PERSON PLAY THE ROLES OF PRODUCT OWNER AND
SCRUM MASTER ON THE SCRUM TEAM?

* There is no specific recommendation from *The Scrum Guide* on this. However, based on my experience, for checks and balances, it is better to separate the two roles so two different individuals perform them. The Product Owner is a business-facing person involved in maximization of value delivered in every Sprint. The Scrum Master is the protector of the Development Team, ensuring that the Development Team works at a sustainable pace.
* If the person wears the Product Owner hat often, the Development Team might be pressured to achieve more than what it can handle in the Sprint.
* Similarly, if the person wears the Scrum Master hat often, then the Development Team may not commit enough work, or it may focus on things that technically interest its members rather than on what business demands.

Scrum Events

• • •

SCRUM HAS FIVE FORMAL EVENTS. The Sprint is an overall container event in which the four other formal events of Sprint Planning, Daily Scrum, Sprint Review, and Sprint Retrospective reside. Each event in Scrum is a formal opportunity to inspect and adapt something. These events are designed specifically to provide transparency and enable business Agility. Failure to include any of these events results in reduced transparency and a lost opportunity to inspect and adapt.

Product Backlog refinement is not a formal event of Scrum, but teams are encouraged to do it as it helps with an effective Sprint Planning.

SPRINT

WHAT IS A SPRINT?
The heart of Scrum is the Sprint, a time-box of one month or less during which a "Done," usable, and potentially releasable Product Increment is created.

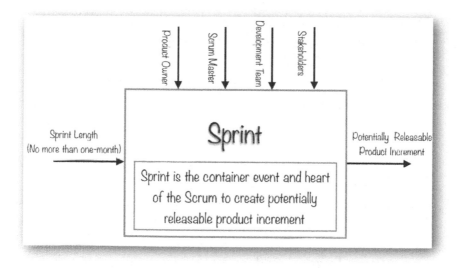

INSIGHTS INTO THE SPRINT

* A Sprint should not be more than one month.
* The next Sprint starts immediately after the completion of the previous Sprint. There are no gaps in between Sprints.
* During the Sprint, no changes are made that would endanger the Sprint goal.
* A first Sprint requires no more than a Product Owner, a team, and enough ideas to potentially complete a full Sprint.
* The Scrum Team crafts the Sprint goal during the Sprint Planning.
* A Sprint can be abnormally terminated or canceled by the Product Owner only. This happens if the Sprint goal becomes obsolete owing to, for example, a change in business conditions.

- At the end of each Sprint, the Development Team must have created at least one piece of functionality that is potentially releasable.
- Each Sprint may be considered a project, and Sprints limit the risks to one calendar month or less.

SPRINT LENGTH

Sprint length determines the heartbeat of all development work, and it is useful for the team to understand how much work can be done during the Sprint.

- Sprint length should be kept constant throughout the release cycle to maintain a steady rhythm of delivery.
- The Sprint time-box must always be respected and should never be extended to meet the forecasted Sprint goal. By doing this, we provide an opportunity for the Development Team to continuously learn and improve on what is really possible to do within a Sprint of this length.
- Scrum recommends the Sprint length be one month or less, during which a "Done," usable, and potentially releasable Product Increment is created. If for some reason you decide to go with a longer Sprint length, Scrum does not stop you from doing that. However, a Sprint length of more than one month increases complexity, reduces focus, and delays getting valuable feedback from the stakeholders.

WHAT ARE SOME FACTORS THAT MUST BE CONSIDERED WHEN DETERMINING THE SPRINT LENGTH?

* Changing market conditions and the frequency at which the requirements change
* The level of uncertainty about the technology
* How often the Scrum Team needs feedback from the Product Owner and customers to ensure that its members are building the "right thing" and the "thing right" the first time
* The duration for which the Scrum Team can stay focused on the goal, the team's maturity, its product knowledge, and the interdependencies with external teams

SPRINT PLANNING

WHAT IS A SPRINT PLANNING?
The Sprint Planning is a meeting involving the entire Scrum Team to collaboratively decide what work will be taken up for the Sprint and how the work will be done.

The Sprint Planning is time-boxed to a maximum of eight hours for a one-month Sprint.

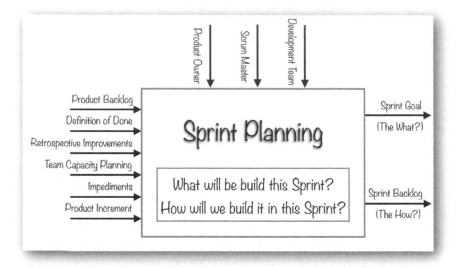

WHAT ARE THE OUTCOMES OF THE SPRINT PLANNING?
The Sprint Planning helps answer two specific questions:

* What can be done in this Sprint?
    * Sprint goal: This gives direction to the Scrum Team, and the team breaks down the selected PBIs from the Product Backlog into an actionable plan, which is the Sprint Backlog.
* How will this goal be accomplished?
    * Sprint Backlog: The selected Sprint Backlog is a forecast by the Development Team of what functionality will be in the next increment and the work needed to deliver that functionality in a "Done" increment.

WHO ATTENDS THE SPRINT PLANNING AND IN WHAT CAPACITY?
All the members of the Scrum Team should participate in the Sprint Planning.

The Scrum Master generally facilitates the meeting. But others in the Scrum Team may also facilitate the meeting, if required.

The Product Owner as a business-facing individual walks through his or her wish list of PBIs that, if implemented in the Sprint, would achieve a business objective. The Product Owner will clarify any questions regarding the PBIs that the team may have. The Product Owner will also make any trade-offs (e.g., business value versus technical feasibility) based on the team's input.

The Scrum Team may invite technical or domain experts external to the team to provide any required input or guidance. The Scrum Team will look at its delivery and performance over previous Sprints, its capacity for the upcoming Sprint, the definition of "Done," and retrospective commitments to increase the accuracy of its forecast during the planning meeting. The cross-functional, self-organizing Development Team pulls a certain amount of work from the Product Backlog that is deemed feasible for the Sprint. The Scrum Team, based on the PBIs pulled from the Product Backlog, crafts a Sprint goal.

HOW DOES ONE CONDUCT AN EFFECTIVE SPRINT PLANNING?
There are many approaches that can be taken to facilitate an effective Sprint Planning. I am listing one approach that I have found effective.

- Prior to the Sprint Planning, the Scrum Team should ensure that the potential PBIs for the Sprint are in "Ready" state: they are ordered, are small enough to be built in one Sprint, have clear acceptance criteria, and possibly have estimates. This can be achieved by conducting regular Product Backlog refinement meetings in the previous Sprint. As a rule of thumb, refinement usually consumes no more than 10 percent of the capacity of the Development Team. Product Backlog refinement is held to ensure that the PBIs for the next Sprint are ready while you are in the current Sprint.

- The Development Team takes one Product Backlog item at a time and collaboratively puts the initial design and plan of the system on the whiteboard. Then the tasks needed to implement the design are identified. This activity can be time-boxed by the Scrum Master to make the Sprint Planning more effective. Each Product Backlog item is broken down into tasks, and possibly each task is given an estimate in hours, and that becomes the Sprint Backlog.

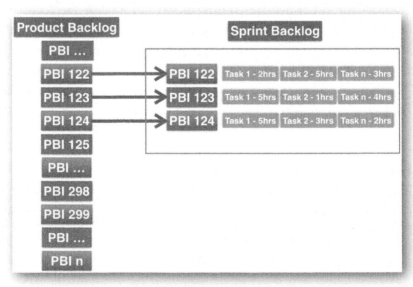

* The Sprint Backlog is a living artifact, and it emerges and changes throughout the Sprint as more detailed level designing happens. New tasks might get added and some existing tasks deleted as more is learned during the implementation of the PBI. It is important to note that a team will rarely be able to identify all the tasks up front. The general guideline is that the Development Team must have enough information for the first few days of the Sprint.

DAILY SCRUM

WHAT IS A DAILY SCRUM?

The Daily Scrum is a fifteen-minute time-boxed event for the Development Team to synchronize Development Team activities, create a plan for the next twenty-four hours, and ensure everyone in the team is aligned toward the Sprint goal.

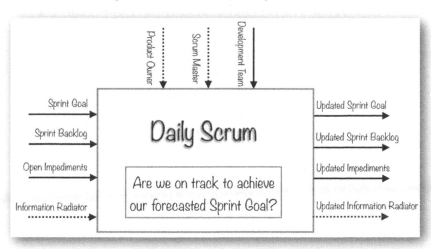

My three-step guideline for an effective Daily Scrum

1. It is recommended to use a physical Scrum board (see Appendix).
   * It will help if the Development Team members ensure that the Scrum board showing the Sprint Backlog or Sprint progress is up to date before the Daily Scrum.
   * Have a clear working agreement for the Daily Scrum, including a start time, agreement that one person speaks at a time, and valuable updates shared between team members.
   * If burn-down charts are used, it is important to understand that they show only the *total* estimate of work remaining across time.
2. Development Team members referencing the Scrum board answer these questions:
   * What did I do yesterday that helped the Development Team meet the Sprint goal?
   * What will I do today to help the Development Team meet the Sprint goal?
   * Do I see any impediment that prevents the Development Team or me from meeting the Sprint goal?
3. The Daily Scrum outcome should be one of these:
   * An updated Sprint goal
   * An updated Sprint Backlog
   * A list of open impediments
   * An updated Scrum board

INSIGHTS INTO THE DAILY SCRUM

* The Daily Scrum is done by inspecting the work done since the last Daily Scrum and forecasting the work that could be done before the next Daily Scrum.
* Daily Scrums help achieve a shared understanding within the Development Team about the next most important activity to be done toward realizing the Sprint goal.
* The Daily Scrum helps improve communication, eliminate other meetings, highlight and promote quick decision making, and improve the Development Team's level of knowledge.
* The Daily Scrum identifies impediments and tracks their resolutions.
* It is mandatory for all the Development Team members to attend the Daily Scrum. The Development Team is responsible for conducting the Daily Scrum. The presence of the Product Owner and the Scrum Master is optional.
* It is a myth that everyone has to stand up in the Daily Scrum. Standing up is just one of the techniques to ensure that the meeting does not go on forever and is time-boxed to fifteen minutes.
* The Daily Scrum is *not* a status meeting for management, and it should *not* be used for detailed discussions or problem resolution.
* The Daily Scrum should be held at the same place and time each day to set a routine that will make it easier for people to follow.
* One of the approaches to facilitate an effective Daily Scrum for inspecting the team's progress toward the Sprint goal

on a daily basis is to have each Development Team member explain the following during the meeting:

* What he or she did yesterday that helped the Development Team meet the Sprint goal
* What he or she will do today to help the Development Team meet the Sprint goal
* Any impediments that could prevent the Development Team or him or her from meeting the Sprint goal

* If the Development Team discovers through a Daily Scrum that they have overcommitted for the Sprint, they will work with the Product Owner to adjust the Sprint scope.
* The Daily Scrum is a fifteen-minute time-boxed event for the Development Team, regardless of the size of the team, and the length of the Sprint.
* The Daily Scrum increases the probability of the Development Team meeting the Sprint goal.

As per The Scrum Guide, the Scrum Master enforces the rule that only Development Team members participate in the Daily Scrum. But won't it help if the Scrum Master and the Product Owner attend the Daily Scrum?
The idea behind making the Development Team the mandatory audience is to ensure the Development Team takes complete ownership of the forecasted Sprint goal and the Sprint Backlog. Daily Scrum fosters shared understanding, responsibility, ownership, self-organizing, empowerment, and quick decision making.

The Scrum Master and the Product Owner are optional attendees for the Daily Scrum, though it is a good practice if they attend as many as they can as long as the presence of the

Scrum Master and Product Owner does not take away the self-organization of the Development Team.

Product Owner participation in the Daily Scrum can be as follows:

* The Product Owner is generally a silent observer when the team members are answering the three questions.
* The Product Owner may speak at the request of the Development Team for any clarification on the forecasted Sprint goal.
* The Product Owner may bring to the notice of the team members any new developments that might impact the Sprint goal, such as changes in the direction of the project and defects newly discovered by customers and proving to be blockers.
* The Product Owner may also suggest to the Development Team that he or she is available for user acceptance testing (UAT) and signing off on any PBI that is completed as per "Done."
* The Product Owner may use the Daily Scrum as an opportunity to cancel the Sprint if the Sprint goal has become obsolete.

It is recommended that the Scrum Master attend the Daily Scrum if the Development Team is new to the Scrum framework to ensure the following:

* The Daily Scrum happens without fail.
* The Development Team is able to time-box the Daily Scrum to fifteen minutes or less.
* Daily Scrums are effective, are self-organized, and add value.

- The Development Team is focused on PBI completion and not just task completion—in other words, the Scrum Master can prevent a Sprint from turning into a mini waterfall.
- The Development Team is protected from external interference during the Daily Scrum.
- Impediments that are stopping the team from making progress toward the Sprint goal are highlighted.

Sprint Review

What is a Sprint Review?

The Sprint Review is a meeting held at the end of the Sprint, before the Sprint time-box expires and prior to the Sprint Retrospective meeting. It is an event where the Scrum Team collaborates with the stakeholders to inspect the Product Increment and collects their feedback. Based on the insights gained, the Product Backlog gets adapted, and collectively the Scrum Team decides on what to build in the upcoming Sprints.

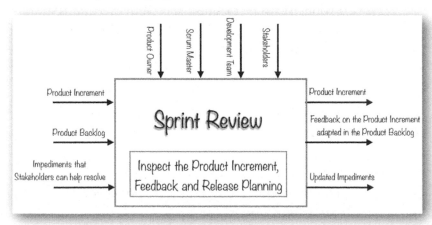

THE FOUR-STEP GUIDELINES FOR AN EFFECTIVE SPRINT REVIEW

1. The Product Owner kicks off the Sprint Review meeting by
   a. reviewing the planned Sprint goal and what the team has accomplished.
2. The Scrum Team inspects the Product Increment with the stakeholders by
   a. discussing the approach to achieving the Sprint goal,
   b. reviewing the challenges faced and how they were resolved, and
   c. inspecting the Product Increment and answering any questions.
3. The Product Owner discusses the latest Product Backlog and likely completion date.
4. The Scrum Team and stakeholders collaborate by
   a. determining what to build in the upcoming Sprint.

INSIGHTS INTO THE SPRINT REVIEW

* Attendees include the Scrum Team and stakeholders invited by the Product Owner.
* Based on what was done and any changes to the Product Backlog (e.g., changing market conditions, new high-priority features, the feedback on the Product Increment) during the Sprint, attendees collaborate on the next things that could be done to optimize value.
* The increment reviewed at the Sprint Review must be usable and adhere to the definition of "Done" so that the Product Owner may choose to release it immediately if required by the business.

* A Product Owner engages actively and regularly with the stakeholders. However, to limit the disturbance to the development progress and keep focus high, the stakeholders have a formal role in the process only during the Sprint Review.

* The Product Owner maintains transparency by using the Sprint Review as an opportunity to present changes in the Product Backlog during the Sprint to the stakeholders. He also uses the opportunity to assess progress toward completing projected work by the desired time for the goal and keeps the stakeholders abreast of the latest information.

* In the Sprint Review meeting, a working functionality increment is demonstrated with the main intention to elicit feedback from the stakeholders who are present.

* This is a four-hour time-boxed meeting for one-month Sprints. For shorter Sprints, the event is usually shorter.

THE SCRUM TEAM DOES NOT HAVE ANYTHING TO SHOW AT THE SPRINT REVIEW. CAN THE SPRINT REVIEW BE CANCELED?
No. The Sprint Review is a mandatory event in the Scrum. No matter what the outcome of the Sprint is, the Sprint Review cannot be canceled.

It is important for the Scrum Team to understand that the Sprint Review is an excellent opportunity for inspection and adaptation even in the absence of a Product Increment. The feedback from the stakeholders can determine the course of action for the next Sprint.

SPRINT RETROSPECTIVE

WHAT IS A SPRINT RETROSPECTIVE?
The Sprint Retrospective is a formal opportunity for the Scrum Team to inspect itself and create a plan for improvements to be enacted during the next Sprint.

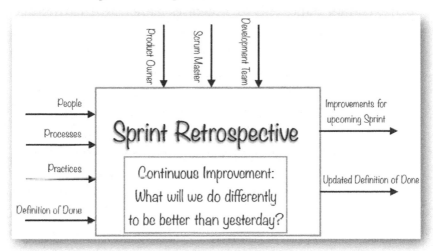

THE SIX-STEP GUIDELINES FOR AN EFFECTIVE SPRINT RETROSPECTIVE

1. **Start with appreciation.** Open the floor for the Scrum Team members to appreciate each other's work. The appreciation has to be genuine.

2. **Make improvements from the last Sprint Retrospective.** Did the team successfully put the improvement in practice? If not, the retrospective discussion needs to be steered toward that.

3. **Set the stage**. The retrospective has to be time bound and fact based with no room for perceptions. This allows Scrum Team members to have a common reference and sets a good platform for an effective retrospective. The Scrum Master normally facilitates this, and it is critically important that the facilitator be neutral and not influence others with his or her thoughts.

4. **Gather data**. This step involves gathering data from the participants. There are many ways in which the data can be collected. Some options include using Post-its; gathering data anonymously; conducting an open discussion; engaging in theme-based communication, collaboration, or decision making; and discussing an unmet goal or feedback for the Scrum Master or Product Owner.

5. **Generate insights.** Generate insights from the data collected by categorizing and eliminating duplicates. Discuss what worked well, and ensure that the Scrum Team intends to continue doing the same. Identify areas of improvements, and order the improvement areas based on value. Here are two useful tips:

   a. Pick two or three improvement areas for a one-month Sprint. Do not try to fix all the areas that need improvement.

   b. Create a backlog of improvements that were raised during the Sprint Retrospectives but were not picked up so far, and maintain/track it somewhere.

6. **Identify the root cause and an improvement plan.** Once the improvement areas have been identified, find the root cause of the problem. The Five Whys technique can be used to deduce the root cause. For example, one of the

improvement areas is the Sprint Planning. Let's find the root cause for this problem.

* Why was the Sprint Planning poor?
    * Well, we did not have a clear objective, and the PBIs were not "Ready."
* Why were the PBIs not "Ready"?
    * The team did not meet for Product Backlog refinement meetings.
* Why did the team not meet?
    * We were supposed to meet on Thursday from four to six o'clock, but the CEO called for an impromptu all hands at the same time.
* Why wasn't the meeting rescheduled?
    * There is no owner for the meeting.

So the real root cause for the poor Sprint Planning was no accountability for the Product Backlog refinement meetings.

It is very important to identify the root cause, come up with action items for improvement, identify an accountable person from the Scrum Team, and agree on the expected time frame for putting the improvements into practice.

INSIGHTS INTO THE SPRINT RETROSPECTIVE

* The Scrum Team inspects and reflects on all aspects of work: technology, social aspects, the Scrum process, people, development practices, tools, product quality, definition of "Done," and so on.

- During each Sprint Retrospective, the Scrum Team plans ways to increase product quality by adapting the definition of "Done" as appropriate.
- The Product Owner participates in the retrospective as a Scrum Team member.
- The Sprint Retrospective meeting is basically about establishing what went well, where there is room for improvement, and what experiments might be usefully conducted in order to learn and build a better product.
- The Sprint Retrospective occurs after the Sprint Review and prior to the next Sprint Planning.
- This is a three-hour time-boxed meeting for one-month Sprints. For shorter Sprints, the event is usually shorter.
- The Sprint Retrospective is a private event for the Scrum Team. External influences like stakeholders, managers, and others outside the Scrum Team must not attend the Sprint Retrospective.

PRODUCT BACKLOG REFINEMENT

Product Backlog refinement is a good practice to collaboratively manage the Product Backlog, and the PBIs acquire a degree of transparency through refinement activities. Refinement helps the Development Team more easily create a forecast of work for the Sprint during the Sprint Planning.

However, refinement is not one of the official time-boxed Scrum events.

The Product Owner represents the stakeholders in the Scrum Team.

He collaborates with the stakeholders, user communities, and product managers to identify the most important product requirements and adds them to the Product Backlog and refines them.

Product Backlog refinement is an ongoing process. This typically requires active interaction with the Development Team for the Product Owner to convey, stress, and clarify the stakeholders' needs to the Scrum Team. The Product Owner and the Development Team collaborate on the details of PBIs that likely will be worked on in the next few Sprints.

The detailing helps the Scrum Team limit the turbulence that is usually experienced in the first few days of the upcoming Sprint. It tries to reveal dependencies, understand better what is expected from that PBI, decide on the shared approach for its development, and help the Product Owner understand the reasoning behind the estimates of the effort needed and the development impact at the functional level. The refinement also further assists the Product Owner in ordering the PBIs.

The Product Owner and the Development Team refine the PBIs in one or two Sprints prior to the Sprint in which they likely will be worked on.

Refinement may also happen in the same Sprint if they were not able to do it in the preceding Sprints.

As noted in *The Scrum Guide*, refinement usually consumes no more than 10 percent of a Development Team's Sprint capacity.

The relationship and the trust established between the Product Owner and the Development Team generally determine the time needed for refinement. If the Development Team and Product Owner are OK with less precise PBIs, the Product Owner and the Development Team do not have to spend a lot of time on refinement.

Multiple Scrum Teams that are working off the same Product Backlog and are continually dependent on each other can ensure that appropriate representatives from both teams are present during the Product Backlog refinement.

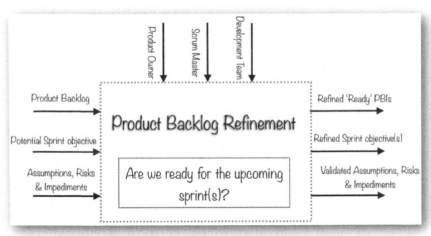

TIME BOX OF EACH SCRUM EVENT

Event	Duration
Sprint	A horizon of no more than one month
Sprint Planning	Eight-hour time-boxed meeting for one month Sprints. For shorter Sprints, the event is usually shorter.
Daily Scrum	15-minute time-boxed event
Sprint Review	Four-hour time-boxed meeting for one-month Sprints. For shorter Sprints, the event is usually shorter.
Sprint Retrospective	Three-hour time-boxed meeting for one-month Sprints. For shorter Sprints, the event is usually shorter.
Product Backlog Refinement (Optional)	Consumes no more than 10% of the capacity of the Development Team.

Scrum Artifacts

• • •

PRODUCT BACKLOG

THE PRODUCT BACKLOG IS AN ordered list of everything that might be needed in the product and is the single source of requirements for the product. It evolves as the product and the environment in which it will be used evolves. Backlog items higher on the list have more clarity and details than the ones below. As long as a product exists, its Product Backlog also exists.

Scrum Teams must frequently inspect Scrum artifacts and progress to detect undesirable variances. The Product Backlog is the primary tool and a living artifact that is actively maintained and updated to reflect reality and is kept transparent for all the stakeholders by the Product Owner. At the Sprint Review, attendees collaborate on the next things that could be done to optimize value, which are processed into an updated Product Backlog.

The Product Backlog is dynamic; it constantly changes to identify what the product needs in order to be appropriate, competitive, and useful. PBIs can be updated at any time by the Product Owner or at the Product Owner's discretion.

- One product has one Product Backlog and one Product Owner. One or more Scrum Teams can work off the same Product Backlog.
- Ordering the Product Backlog helps teams maximize the business value delivered. The most important items are always on top of the Product Backlog. Ordering is in general based primarily on effort, value, dependencies, and risk. The Product Owner is accountable for ordering the Product Backlog. Value is likely to vary across products and organizations.
- The Product Backlog is an ordered list of PBIs. PBIs can be in the form of nonfunctional requirements, new features, defects, use cases, defects, technical debt, and so on.
- The PBI implementation is considered complete when there is no further work remaining to be done on the item to be released.
- The Product Backlog is the road map in Scrum. It is a living artifact that grows and changes as and when more is learned about the evolving product and its customers.
- The Product Backlog is one single source of truth. All requirements for the changes to the product by the Development Team(s) must ultimately originate from the Product Backlog.
- The PBIs pulled into the Sprint have to be small enough to be built in one Sprint.

SPRINT BACKLOG

The Sprint Backlog is the set of PBIs selected for the Sprint, plus a plan, often a list of tasks, for delivering the Product Increment and realizing the Sprint goal.

The Sprint Backlog is a highly visible, real-time picture of the work and single point of truth that is owned and maintained only by the Development Team and covers what the team plans to accomplish during the Sprint.

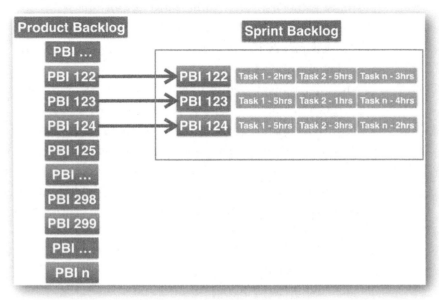

* The Sprint Backlog is the Development Team's work plan (PBIs and the plan) for the Sprint and is created in the Sprint Planning.
* The Sprint Backlog can consist of tests, tasks, use cases, user stories, nonfunctional requirements, experiments, and so on.
* The Development Team owns the Sprint Backlog and modifies the Sprint Backlog throughout the Sprint. The Sprint Backlog emerges throughout the Sprint.
* As the Sprint progresses, the Sprint Backlog gets updated with new work items as soon as they are identified.

PRODUCT INCREMENT

- The increment is the cumulative sum of all the PBIs completed during the Sprint and the value of the increments of all previous Sprints.
- At the end of the Sprint, the increment must be in a "Done" state, which is to say that it must be integrated into the existing Product Increment during the Sprint and collectively it must be a potentially releasable increment that meets the definition of "Done."
- The Product Owner decides on releasing the Product Increment to production when it makes sense.

SPRINT GOAL

- The Product Owner generally comes to the Sprint Planning with a business objective in mind. After the Development Team forecasts the PBIs it will deliver in the Sprint, the Scrum Team crafts a Sprint goal.
- The Sprint goal gives direction to the Scrum Team, and the team decomposes the selected items from the Product Backlog into an actionable plan, the Sprint Backlog.
- During the Sprint no changes are made that would endanger the Sprint goal.
- Some examples of good Sprint goals are the following:
    - Support the application on Internet Explorer in addition to the Chrome browser.
    - Improve the performance of the application by 30 percent.

Artifact Transparency

• • •

Definition of "Done"

When a Product Backlog item or an increment is described as "Done," everyone on the Scrum Team must have a shared understanding of what "Done" means, to ensure transparency. This is the definition of "Done" for the Scrum Team and is used to assess when work is complete on the Product Increment. The increment reviewed at the Sprint Review must be potentially releasable so a Product Owner may choose to immediately release it.

Here is a sample definition of "Done":

1. All acceptance criteria for the PBI must pass.
2. Sign-off for the PBI must happen in a clean environment.
3. Seventy percent of the tests for the PBI must be automated.
4. There must be no Severity 1 or 2 defects for the PBI being signed off on.
5. The unit test code coverage must be at 80 percent.

INSIGHTS INTO THE DEFINITION OF "DONE"

* The definition of "Done" is created and owned by the Development Team. The "Done" criteria guide the Development Team in creating a forecast at the Sprint Planning. If the organization has specific quality expectations, the Development Team should know them.

* The definition of "Done" enables empiricism as it creates transparency over the Product Increment inspected at the Sprint Review. The Development Team, the Product Owner, and the Scrum Master are all in alignment, as they clearly understand what it takes for a Product Increment to be ready for release.

* The definition of "Done"
  * creates a shared understanding of what is releasable software and
  * guides the Development Team in the Sprint Planning on how many PBIs it can pick from the Product Backlog.

* Nonfunctional requirements can be added to each PBI, but at times they are forgotten, which results in missed opportunities. To overcome this issue it might be a good idea to add nonfunctional requirements to the definition of "Done" so that the team remembers to take care of them every Sprint.

* A mature Scrum Team inspects its definition of "Done" at every Sprint Retrospective and looks for opportunities to raise its quality bar by improving its definition of "Done" by making it more stringent.

* A good definition of "Done" can help reduce the release stabilization time, reduce the total cost of ownership (TCO), and reduce the technical debt.
* Nonadherence to the agreed definition of "Done" by the Development Team generally results in increased technical debt as it creates false assumptions about the actual state of the system. In addition, releasing a suboptimal-quality product might also result in customer escalations and dissatisfaction.

HOW DOES THE DEFINITION OF "DONE" GUIDE THE DEVELOPMENT TEAM IN KNOWING HOW MANY PBIS IT CAN SELECT DURING A SPRINT PLANNING?
By agreeing upon the definition of "Done," the Scrum Team defines the quality of the Product Increment that will be available at the end of each Sprint.

The definition of "Done" is all the things that the Development Team has agreed to do, in addition to meeting the defined acceptance criteria for each PBI, to ensure that the potentially releasable increment is of good quality.

Imagine a very novice Development Team creating a very stringent definition of "Done" that requires this for every PBI:

1. 80 percent unit test case coverage
2. 100 percent automation of all identified test cases

This novice team is totally new to the concept of automation and writing of unit test cases. In this scenario, because they have committed to the above for every PBI, the number of PBIs the Development Team can pick up for the Sprint will be constrained.

However, consider that the same team has this as the definition of "Done":

1. 20 percent unit test case coverage
2. 50 percent automation of all identified test cases

The Development Team might be able to pick more PBIs in the Sprint, but eventually they will slow down, as they will be spinning manual regression testing cycles for the previously completed PBIs.

The definition of "Done" generally becomes more and more stringent as the Scrum Team matures.

HOW SHOULD MULTIPLE SCRUM TEAMS DELIVER A "DONE," POTENTIALLY RELEASABLE INCREMENT FOR A PRODUCT IN A SPRINT?
Two of the most important concerns for multiple Development Teams working from the same Product Backlog are

* minimizing the dependencies between the teams and
* integrating their work to deliver a single potentially releasable software increment.

When multiple Development Teams are working on a single product, they must agree on a common definition of "Done." This definition of "Done" should enable their integrated increments to be potentially shippable. The Development Teams on all of the Scrum Teams must mutually define the definition of "Done."

In addition, the Development Teams coordinate their work to deliver a single increment. They also integrate their work before the end of the Sprint.

For example, let's say there are five Scrum Teams.

Team	Items in definition of "Done"
1	A, C, G, H, I, J, Z
2	A, B, M, N, J, Z
3	A, C, K, P, J, Z
4	A, B, M, L, J, Z
5	A, D, M, L, J, Z

Common definition of "Done" for all 5 Teams
A, J, Z

For example, item Z: Integrate the "Done" increment with the "Done" increments of the other Scrum Teams.

The mutually agreed common definition of "Done" for the integrated increment by all Scrum Teams will be A, J, and Z. In addition to the common definition of "Done," all teams must also adhere to their own definitions of "Done."

For example, Team 1 for common integrated "Done" at a bare minimum will complete items A, J, and Z for each PBI. However, Team 1 is bit more mature and is able to do items C,

G, H, and I as per its "Done" criteria. It must continue doing that.

The ultimate goal of all Scrum Teams must be to make the common "Done" more stringent and uniform across all teams.

Thus, for each Sprint, all Scrum Teams have a "Done" increment that integrates with all of the other "Done" increments from all other Scrum Teams. The sum of all increments is the increment for that Sprint.

It is also important to understand that Scrum does not require all the Scrum Teams working on the same product to have the same Sprint length. In practice, this means if any team is on a four-week cadence, other teams can Sprint on one- or two-week cadences. If any team is on a three-week cadence, other teams are limited to one- or three-week cadences. The team with the longest Sprint cadence is when all Scrum Teams will have a single cumulative integrated potentially releasable "Done" Product Increment.

Self-Organization

• • •

WHAT IS SELF-ORGANIZATION?

"KNOWLEDGE WORKERS HAVE TO MANAGE themselves. They have to have autonomy," says Peter Drucker.

HOW DOES SCRUM PROMOTE SELF-ORGANIZATION?

1. By specifying a lightweight framework: three roles, five events, and three artifacts.
2. By removing titles for the Development Team members. Everyone is equal, and there is no hierarchy within the Development Team.
3. By empowering the Development Team and determining the best way to accomplish its work.

Self-organization enables

* creativity within the Scrum Teams,
* accountability in the Scrum Team, and

* people's personal commitments to achieving the goals of the Scrum Team.

Self-organization is something that cannot be imposed on the team. Self-organization does not mean a free run where Development Team members can do whatever they desire. Self-organization happens by setting clear boundaries within which the empowered team members can organize their own work. Some factors that promote self-organization are the following:

* Trust: People in the team must be able to trust each other, communicate freely, achieve insights, and collaborate. Anything that is a barrier to achieving these should be removed.
* Time-boxing: This Scrum rule helps focus and manage risks.
* Fixed Sprint length: This factor helps with the consistent delivery of business value in every time-boxed Sprint.
* Optimal Development Team size: A cross functional Development Team of three to nine members, as recommended in *The Scrum Guide*, helps remove unnecessary complexity and communication overhead.
* Definition of "Done": Creating transparency regarding the work inspected during the Sprint Review, it also enables everyone in the Scrum Team to have common shared understanding.
* Scrum Values: The Scrum values of courage, focus, commitment, respect, and openness are embodied and lived by everyone.

What Are Some Signs That Teams Are Self-Organizing?

1. Development team members collaboratively select and re-plan their own work during the Sprint.
2. The work identified in the Sprint Backlog created by the Development Team ensures that the definition of "Done" will be met.
3. No one tells the Development Team how to turn PBIs into a potentially releasable increment.

How Does Time-Boxing Promote Self-Organization?

1. Time boxes help get everyone aligned and focused on the Sprint goal with a common objective of creating a potentially releasable Product Increment that adheres to the definition of "Done" by the end of each Sprint.
2. Time boxes encourage the Development Team members who are doing hands-on work on the problem to create the best possible outcome in the time allotted and within the current context.
3. Time boxes are like guardrails. They make the team safe by restricting the risk.

How Do the Scrum Roles Promote Self-Organization?

The Scrum Team consists of three distinct roles: the Scrum Master, the Product Owner, and the Development Team. The accountability of each role complements the accountability of the other roles. Hence, collaboration between these roles is the key to success:

* The **Scrum Master**, through servant-leadership, coaches, facilitates, educates, and guides the team to solve its own problems by using the three pillars of empiricism. The Scrum Master understands that constructive disagreements are necessary to build high-performing teams. The Scrum Master allows the team to learn from the cycle of failing, trying, and failing again. The Scrum Master also helps self-organization by proactively and uncompromisingly removing impediments that are beyond the team's self-organization capability.

* The **Product Owner** closely interacts with stakeholders and product management to identify the most valuable work. The Product Owner relies on the Development Team for the actual delivery of a potentially shippable software increment in every Sprint. At every Sprint Review, the stakeholders help the team in shaping the future product.

* The **Development Team** members collaboratively select their own work from the Product Backlog ordered by the Product Owner. They collaboratively create actionable activities to realize their forecast as reflected in the Sprint Backlog. They replan their work on a daily basis within the time-boxed Sprint to optimize the team's output. They deliver a potentially releasable increment (integrated with increments of other teams, if multiple teams are involved) of software at the end of each Sprint. This self-directedness, the ability for people to direct their own work, motivates them and reinforces self-organization.

One of the best examples of self-organization comes straight from Ken Schwaber's blog post "Self-Organization and Our Belief That We Are in Charge."

Schwaber, K., (July 2012). kenschwaber.wordpress.com/2012/07/25/self-organization-and-our-belief-that-we-are-in-charge/

"I pose the following question to Scrum Masters: What is the best way to organize 100 developers into Scrum Teams?"

According to Ken, he would

let the developers self-organize themselves into Development Teams as per the recommendation in *The Scrum Guide* that has all the cross-functional skills to build an integrated done Increment every Sprint. The Scrum Master may remind them that all one hundred people must be engaged meaningfully and that mentoring is expected. The Scrum Master may have the lead developers lead a discussion about the software and architecture to be worked on, with the underlying dependencies. The Scrum Master may have the Product Owner discuss the intricacies of the Product Backlog. And, if they organize sub-optimally, they can correct and continually adjust team membership as they find out more. Promote a learning organization with Bottom-up intelligence. So the one-hundred-people group self-organizes and divides itself into teams.

Myths, Mysteries, and Misconceptions of Scrum

• • •

WHAT ARE SPRINT 0, HARDENING SPRINTS, RELEASE SPRINTS, AND STABILIZATION SPRINTS?

SHORT ANSWER: SCRUM DOES NOT have terms like Sprint 0, Hardening Sprint, Release Sprint, and Stabilization Sprint in its vocabulary. The heart of Scrum is a Sprint, a time box of one month or less during which a "Done," usable, and potentially releasable Product Increment is created. Each Sprint is a project used to accomplish something.

IS SCRUM A METHODOLOGY OR A FRAMEWORK?

Scrum is not a methodology. It is a framework within which you can employ various processes and techniques.

A methodology is a set of values, principles, tools, and practices that can be used to guide processes to achieve a particular goal. Methodologies are generally prescriptive and have very strictly defined sets of processes. Methodologies also have a high level of predictability and possibly a repeatable outcome.

Frameworks are lightweight, more like blueprints with minimal prescription and guidance that leave room for other practices and tools to be included but provide the bare minimal processes required. Scrum as a framework of minimal prescriptions describes roles and rules, based on Agile values and principles, through which small cross-functional teams frequently deliver valuable, potentially releasable Product Increments. The prescriptions are minimal, but every single one of them addresses a common dysfunction of software development.

Based on my experience, I have seen successful Agile adoptions start with Scrum as a foundation. The Scrum framework is then complemented with solid engineering practices like continuous integration and deployment, test automation, pair programming, code reviews, refactoring, coding and architectural standards, and test-driven development to help deliver a high-quality Product Increment in every Sprint. The Scrum foundation along with engineering practices could be further complemented with Lean practices to be even more effective and efficient by reducing the cycle time of feature delivery.

MY DESIGNATION IS DEVELOPMENT MANAGER. DOES THIS MEAN I HAVE NO ROLE IN SCRUM?

Scrum knows only three roles: the Product Owner, the Scrum Master, and the Development Team. In Scrum, the Development Team self-organizes. There is no formal role called "manager" to oversee what the Development Team members are doing on a daily basis and assign tasks to Development Team members. This does not mean that there is no room for managers.

Managers can be change agents to promote Agility and empiricism in the organization. They can help the team remove organizational impediments that the Scrum Masters are having difficulty resolving. They can be guardians of the Scrum process.

They can be coaches, mentors, and teachers for the Scrum Masters, Product Owners, and the Development Team. Depending on their skills and traits, they can play the role of either Scrum Master or Product Owner or even transition into Development Team members if they have the necessary skills.

Scrum knows no role called project manager, program manager, development managers, or chief product owner.

How Is Architecture Handled in Agile?

Scrum embraces the Agile principle of emergent architecture and design. Architectural needs emerge due to functional and nonfunctional requirements. Certain nonfunctional requirements like security, deployment platforms, compliance, and scalability are often of very high value and ordered high in the Product Backlog. Usually some parts of each of those nonfunctional requirements are required for an initial release of a minimum viable product. Business-facing functionality (i.e., functional requirements) also drives architectural and design needs as well. In Scrum, each Sprint serves to build at least one piece of business-facing functionality that has at least some tiny amount of value. So as we evolve the system, we build only enough architecture and design to support the functional and nonfunctional requirements that we are focusing on for that Sprint. Just remember: at a minimum we have to build at least one piece of that business-facing functionality, regardless of how many nonfunctional requirements and architecture we are also focusing on. Then with every subsequent Sprint, more and more of the architecture and design emerges in response to more and more high-ordered requirements. The purpose of this is to build architecture and design only in response to the highest-valued requirements at the top of the Product Backlog.

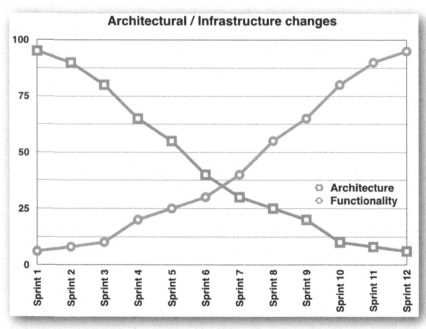

In the example shown in the chart above, in Sprint 1 the majority of the work done by the Scrum Team is on architecture/infrastructure; however, enough business-facing valuable functionality is still released by the team to deliver value and validate the current architecture work. As the team progresses further Sprint over Sprint, the architectural needs decrease, and the value-driven business functionality delivered increases.

The Development Team also ensures good architecture by ensuring a set of guiding architectural principles that every Development Team member understands and follows while writing code. In addition, architecture is an ongoing discussion in the Development Team focusing on implementing current Sprint Backlog items.

My fellow Scrum.org trainer, Charles Bradley, shares an additional example of emergent architecture, which is available in the Appendix.

One Scrum Team Is Currently Developing a Product. What Impact Will It Have on Its Productivity When One More Scrum Team Is Deployed in This Product Development Effort?

The productivity of the original Scrum Team is likely to decrease because it might do the following:

* Run into dependencies between PBIs, which might have to be resolved
* Face integration challenges, as the team has to create an integrated Product Increment by the end of the Sprint working together with the new team
* Have to be involved in knowledge sharing that might consume its capacity further

WHAT ARE COMMONLY OBSERVED SCRUM MYTHS, MYSTERIES, AND MISCONCEPTIONS?

* Scrum Teams are assigned to several projects or features. This results in context switching (i.e., multitasking), and the outcome is increased cycle time and delayed value delivery to business.

* The software is not released to market frequently, thereby missing the opportunity to gather customer feedback.

* When Scrum Teams say "Done," they are not really "Done." They need additional regression test cycles, or they need additional cycles to integrate their work with the work of other teams.

* There is more than one Product Owner for one product with no clear accountability.

* Proxy Product Owners are assigned to the Scrum Team with no empowerment to make business decisions, resulting in unnecessary delays.

* The role of the Scrum Master is undermined by assigning a part-time Scrum Master or team members taking turns to play the role of a Scrum Master in every Sprint.

* Instead of recruiting someone with experience in working with Scrum, organizations recruit someone with no prior Scrum experience or send their in-house project managers to a two-day Scrum class, hoping they can play the role of an effective Scrum Master.

* There is a mini waterfall within the Sprint—for example, not limiting the work in progress for the PBIs and keeping the testing toward the end of the Sprint.

- There is command and control by the Scrum Master or Product Owner. The Product Owner dictates Implementation details.

- There are Sprints called Sprint 0, Design Sprint, Architectural Sprint, Hardening Sprint, Stabilization Sprint, and Testing Sprint.

- There is a certain myth that burn-down charts, burn-up charts, and cumulative-flow diagrams must be used by the Scrum Teams as metrics. The Scrum framework does not prescribe any of these metrics. Depending on the value these metrics drive, you can choose to use them or drop them altogether.

- It is a myth that success of the team can be measured by an increase in the team's velocity. Velocity is neither good nor bad. It is just a metric that can be handy for planning. It is a metric to measure capacity, not productivity.

- There are Sprints after Sprints just to build the overall architecture with no real business functionality at the end of each Sprint.

- There are geographically distributed Scrum Teams with members on different continents. Many times this is an unavoidable reality, but understand that the quantity and the quality of spontaneous communication decrease drastically, thereby resulting in miscommunications, delays, redundancy in work being performed, reduced focus, and so on.

- The Development Team, instead of collaborating closely with the Product Owner, looks for a detailed specification and requirements document.

* Organizations do not adhere to the minimally defined Scrum framework of three roles, five events, and three artifacts. At times they skip events like Daily Scrum, Sprint Planning, Sprint Review, and Sprint Retrospective, thereby missing important inspection and adaptation opportunities.

A Case Study on Scrum-Based Product Development

• • •

LET'S SAY A SCRUM TEAM was building an e-mail application very similar to Gmail for one of its customers. The customer was very happy with the progress the team had made so far on the product development front.

The customer then came up with an idea for a new feature for the product. He wanted to build a filtering capability in the e-mail application. The filtering functionality would display only the e-mails that the customer cared about. He was very excited and hoped that this feature would be implemented as soon as possible.

As a next step, the Product Owner and Development Team members collaborated and brainstormed to identify the different ways in which e-mail could be filtered. Here are some options they came up with for filtering:

* By sender
* By recipient

- By subject
- By date
- By keyword
- By attachment
- By size
- By spam
- By junk

The Product Owner was happy with the outcome of the brain-storming session and was hoping that all these features would get implemented in the following Sprint as per customer request.

The team came up with initial size estimates of the PBIs and forecasted that each PBI would take one Sprint of one week to build.

The Product Owner was a bit disappointed that his customer would have to wait multiple Sprints for the entire feature to be ready, but he trusted his Development Team's estimates.

The Product Owner worked closely with the customer and explained the situation to him. However, the Product Owner informed the customer that the Development Team would deliver a usable software increment in every Sprint. The customer felt a bit comfortable with this statement of the Product Owner.

The Product Owner then requested the customer order the Product Backlog according to the defined business value. Together, they ordered the Product Backlog in terms of business value (i.e., highest business value item on the top).

* By date
* By keyword
* By attachment
* By sender
* By recipient
* By subject
* By size
* By spam
* By junk

It was very clear to the Development Team that the "Filtering E-Mails by Date Range" function was at the top of the Product Backlog and that is what the Product Owner wanted them to build first.

However, it was still a one-line requirement, and it was not "Ready" for the Development Team to pull from the Product Backlog and start implementing. It was not "Ready," because the acceptance criteria for the PBI were missing, and they also had to be sure that the PBI could be completed in one Sprint. The Scrum Team collaborated as part of the Product Backlog refinement meeting and ensured the PBI was in "Ready" state by adding the acceptance criteria and slicing the PBI enough for it to be completed in one Sprint.

An example of a PBI in "Ready" state

PBI 1: "As an e-mail user, I want to filter e-mails using a specific date range so that I can see exactly the e-mails I am interested in."

Acceptance criteria for the PBI:

1. The "From" date should not be greater than the "To" date.
2. All dates must be entered in DD/MM/YYYY format.
3. A calendar pop-up must be provided for selecting the date range.
4. For the selected date range, the first twenty e-mails must be displayed, and an option of pagination must be provided for the remaining e-mails in the selected date range.

The Development Team at this point had enough information to implement the PBI as it was in "Ready" state.

The Sprint lasted for one week. It started on Monday and ended on Friday, effectively giving the team five days to build the potentially releasable unit of software.

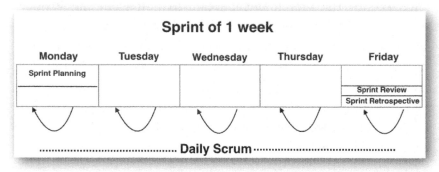

The Scrum Team met Monday morning and had a Sprint Planning meeting. By the end of the Sprint Planning, the Scrum Team had forecasted what they could build for this Sprint. The objective was to filter e-mails by date range, and that became their Sprint goal.

In addition, the Development Team had put a plan together by putting on the whiteboard a high-level design for how they planned to implement the PBI, and this was reflected in their Sprint Backlog.

During the Sprint Planning, the Development Team realized that they had underestimated the effort needed to build the feature "Filtering E-Mails by Date Range." The team had identified that they did not have canned APIs available for the calendar pop-up for the "From" and "To" date text boxes and that building the APIs would take additional effort.

The Development Team brought this to the attention of the Product Owner. The Product Owner reviewed the acceptance criteria and suggested that the customer would be happy to enter the date manually in "DD/MM/YYYY" format and he could move the calendar pop-up as a new PBI that could be addressed in a future Sprint, thereby reducing the scope of the PBI. The Development Team was happy with the suggestion and carried on with its planning meeting, taking into account the new changes suggested by the Product Owner. This activity is what is called story slicing.

The Development Team met together daily for not more than fifteen minutes, starting at eleven o'clock, to conduct its Daily Scrum. The Daily Scrum was done to ensure team members were aligned with the plan to achieve the Sprint goal.

The Development Team regularly kept the Product Owner informed on the progress it had made toward the Sprint goal. The

Product Owner in turn kept the customer informed about what he could expect to see in the upcoming Sprint Review.

As advised in *The Scrum Guide*, during the Sprint the team also met for Product Backlog refinement to refine the Product Backlog item for the following Sprint. The team members refined the "Filtering E-Mails by Keyword" PBI.

PBI 2: "As an e-mail user, I want to filter e-mails using keywords so that I can see exactly the e-mails I am interested in."

The Product Owner scheduled a Sprint Review meeting at three o'clock on Friday. The Product Owner took the liberty of inviting the customer to the Sprint Review meeting to inspect the increment and gather feedback from him. Before coming to this meeting, the Product Owner had already signed off the "Filtering E-Mails by Date Range" PBI since the team had met all the acceptance criteria, and he was satisfied with the outcome.

The team demonstrated to the customer the date-range filtering feature that they built in the Sprint. The customer was happy with the outcome but had some feedback about the look-and-feel aspect of the implementation. The Product Owner captured the feedback provided by the client in the Product Backlog as a new PBI. The customer then requested the Product Owner put the completed PBI into production, as his customers would be delighted to get the option to filter e-mails by date range.

The customer then requested the team build additional filtering PBIs for the product. The customer also confirmed that the next feature to be built was "Filtering E-Mails by Keyword." The team agreed.

After the Sprint Review, the Scrum Team got together for the Sprint Retrospective, a formal opportunity for the Scrum Team to inspect itself and create a plan for improvements to be enacted during the next Sprint. By the end of the retrospective, the team had identified an improvement. They decided to parallelize the coding and testing activities a bit more. In addition, they also added a new line item to their existing definition of "Done": 70 percent of the planned test cases for the PBI will be automated.

Following this, the team decided to celebrate its Sprint success by treating themselves to ice cream and pizza. The Scrum Master was kind enough to arrange this for the team. The Scrum Team members had a relaxing weekend and were ready for the next Sprint starting on Monday. They were going to build "Filtering E-Mails by Keyword" in this Sprint.

The team met Monday morning at nine o'clock for the next Sprint, beginning with the Sprint Planning, where the team members took into account the improvements from the previous Sprint. They conducted their regular Daily Scrums, and by Friday the team had built the "Filtering E-Mails by Keyword" feature.

The customer attended the Sprint Review and was very content with the addition of the keyword filtering feature to the existing date-range filtering feature. The customer liked what he saw and requested the Product Owner roll out the newly built PBI into production.

The Scrum Team was quite excited about its performance so far, and its members were looking forward to build the third PBI, "Filtering E-Mails by Attachment," in the third Sprint.

But the customer did not want any additional PBIs related to the filtering feature in the Product Backlog anymore. He told the Scrum Team that his users were more than satisfied with the filtering features built so far, and therefore they could start working on a new feature in the pipeline. Thus, the Scrum Team delivered a minimum viable feature (MVF) and lived up to the Agile principle "Simplicity, the art of maximizing the amount of work not done."

AUTHOR'S THOUGHTS
AND CONCLUSION

• • •

BEING AGILE IS A JOURNEY. In my eleven years of Agile experience of working with small, medium, and large enterprise organizations as a trainer and a coach, I have yet to come across a Scrum Team that claims it has reached a nirvana state of Agile—in other words, one that does not have anything to improve on. Some have started the journeys, some are midway, and some are further in their journeys. The secret to being Agile is the team asking this question on daily basis: Are we better than we were yesterday? And having the courage to experiment and try something new if the answer to the above question is no.

Scrum, as in the game of chess, is a lightweight set of rules. Without being prescriptive, it defines the roles and the rules by which the game of Scrum can be played. The organization that has gained a deep understanding of and insights into the roles, rules, and values of Scrum—and makes a sincere attempt to embrace them—has a better chance to master Scrum and gain the benefits Agile has to offer.

To really take in and reap the benefits of Agility in an organization, it is important to have a complete top-down and bottom-up buy-in. Successful teams are the ones that embrace the three pillars of empiricism: transparency, inspection, and adaptation. These teams' members live the Scrum values of focus, commitment, respect, courage, and openness in their day-to-day work, and they understand that their success is measured by consistently delivering significant new value to the business.

Organizations must strive to create teams that believe in innovation and creativity and that are self-organized and self-managed. Then and only then will they reap the maximum benefits that Scrum has to offer.

• • •

Best Practice: Scrum Board, as a Visualization of Sprint Backlog

Scrum Board				
Sprint Goal:	**\<Team Name\>**		Sprint Start Date: dd/mm/yy Sprint End Date: dd/mm/yy	
PBIs for Sprint	To Do	In Progress WIP Limit < x >	Review	Done
Burn-down chart	Impediments Impediment_# | Brief_Text | Severity | Opened_by | Owned_by | ETA		Waste	

EMERGENT ARCHITECTURE: AN EXAMPLE

Here is an example of emergent architecture shared by my fellow Scrum.org trainer, Charles Bradley.

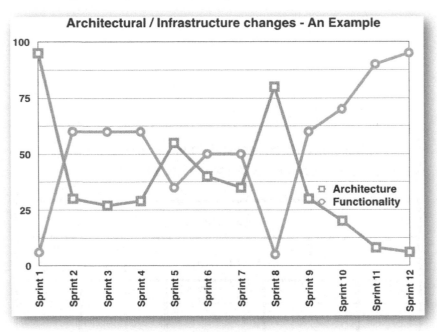

For this team, Sprint 1 included a lot of architecture as it implemented a walking skeleton of the deployment architecture. In addition, the team came to some agreements about good coding practices, test automation, and continuous refactoring so that the code and tests stayed clean and green and remain flexible to change in the future. This would also help prevent technical debt.

In Sprint 1, the team implemented an HTML GUI and a middle-tier server/container and connected to its database via ODBC using straight SQL queries. The team members knew that they would probably improve their architectural implementation choices in later Sprints, but they wanted to get some user feedback on a light architecture at first. In Sprint 1, they implemented some business functionality, which included a log-in screen and an initial dashboard with just a couple of fields on it. In addition to providing some business-facing requirements, this Sprint helped validate the security and deployment platform of the architecture.

Sprints 2–4 focused more on filling out the dashboard and getting some high-value business functionality created. The team obtained some excellent feedback from users. The users were happy but suggested a couple of enhancements that would require much more data to be loaded. The team felt it was time to implement a first-class O/R mapping tool like Hibernate and replace their ODBC queries with that, so Sprint 5 and part of Sprint 6 focused more heavily on that architectural piece and still delivered some business functionality too. Because the team had automated tests surrounding the data-retrieval functionality, it was very easy for them to change this part of the architecture.

Also of note, starting in Sprint 1 and happening in parallel with all of the other work through Sprint 6, the team was working with others in the organization to evaluate and purchase a third-party proprietary component related to its system's primary business domain. It took quite a while to evaluate alternatives, acquire the component, and do the legal legwork around licensing.

Finally, once acquired, during Sprint 8, the team spent a lot of time implementing that third-party component and also producing one tiny piece of initial functionality from that component. It was basic functionality that the users wanted, but its main purpose was to prove that they could successfully connect and use the component for its intended purpose.

After Sprint 8, and in large part owing to the functionality provided by the component, the team was able to churn out a massive amount of functionality. During Sprint 10, the Product Owner felt there was enough functionality to release the initial version of the product, so she released the minimum viable product to a small segment of the users to begin using and providing real-world feedback on.

In this way, the team was able to do emergent architecture, just in time, while also continuing to deliver at least a little bit of business functionality in each Sprint. There are numerous advantages of doing architecture in an emergent way. The team members felt they had a much better feel for the technology and user landscape prior to making architectural choices. Another advantage was that since this was a new product, the team had really gelled, and it was easier for its members to make decisions. One team member also commented about the fact that since implementation was handled immediately after architectural choices, he was able to more efficiently implement them. He recalled that in the past, many of the architectural choices had been made several months before by a totally different group. He felt this approach was much more efficient and effective.

REFERENCES

• • •

Schwaber, K., Sutherland, J. (July 2016). *The Scrum Guide.* scrumguides.org

Scrum.org. (2016). www.scrum.org/Resources.

Scrum.org. (2016). www.scrum.org/Community

Gunther, Verheyen. (Oct 2013). Scrum—a Pocket Guide, a Smart Travel Companion.

Beck, Kent, et al. 2001. Manifesto for Agile Software Development. agilemanifesto.org

Schwaber, K. (July 2012). kenschwaber.wordpress.com/2012/07/25/ self-organization-and-our-belief-that-we-are-in-charge/

Snowded. (July 2014). Cynefin Framework. en.wikipedia.org/wiki/ Cynefin_Framework.

Easter, D., Larsen, D. (July 2006). Agile Retrospectives, Making Good Teams Great.

• • •

Hiren R. Doshi, Scrum.org professional Scrum trainer and coach, is a Scrum enthusiast and an agent for organizational change. Hiren received his bachelor's degree in computer engineering from the University of Pune and his master's degree in computer science from the University of Massachusetts.

Hiren founded Practice Agile Solutions in 2010. He has served as an Agile transformation leader for many organizations, including Sabre Travels, Bank of America, BookMyShow, Tesco, EMC, Morpho, Oracle, Continuum Managed Solutions, Lulu, Germin8, and Aveksa. He has trained over twenty-five hundred students and more than thirty organizations in the use of Scrum.

Hiren has spent the past twenty-one years in professional software development and is experienced in BFSI, storage, online retail and e-commerce, and big data domains. He also blogs about his experiences and speaks at many Agile conferences.

Hiren lives in Mumbai (India) with his wife, Swati, and two daughters, Aditi and Ashwini.

He can be reached at
hirendoshi@practiceagile.com
+91 9619322001
www.practiceagile.com